ANIMAL MOUTHS

David M. Schwartz *is an award-winning author of children's books, on a wide variety of topics, loved by children around the world.* Dwight Kuhn's *scientific expertise and artful eye work together with the camera to capture the awesome wonder of the natural world.*

For a free color catalog describing Gareth Stevens Publishing's list of high-quality books and multimedia programs, call 1-800-542-2595 (USA) or 1-800-461-9120 (Canada). Gareth Stevens Publishing's Fax: (414) 225-0377.

Library of Congress Cataloging-in-Publication Data

Schwartz, David M.
    Animal mouths / by David M. Schwartz; photographs by Dwight Kuhn.
        p. cm. — (Look once, look again)
    Includes bibliographical references (p. 23) and index.
    Summary: Introduces, in simple text and photographs, the mouths of a
puffin, child, housefly, dragonfly nymph, butterfly, chameleon, alligator, and caiman.
    ISBN 0-8368-2425-3 (lib. bdg.)
    1. Mouth—Juvenile literature. [1. Mouth. 2. Animals—Habits and behavior.]
I. Kuhn, Dwight, ill. II. Title. III. Series: Schwartz, David M. Look once, look again.
QL857.S38   1999
573.3'5—dc21   99-18609

This North American edition first published in 1999 by
Gareth Stevens Publishing
1555 North RiverCenter Drive, Suite 201
Milwaukee, Wisconsin 53212 USA

First published in the United States in 1998 by Creative Teaching Press, Inc., P. O. Box 6017, Cypress, California, 90630-0017.

Printed in the United States of America

1 2 3 4 5 6 7 8 9 03 02 01 00 99

ANIMAL MOUTHS

by David M. Schwartz
photographs by Dwight Kuhn

A SPRINGBOARDS INTO
SCIENCE
SERIES

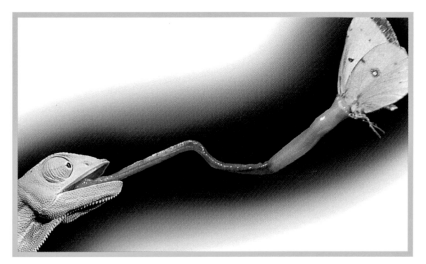

Gareth Stevens Publishing
MILWAUKEE

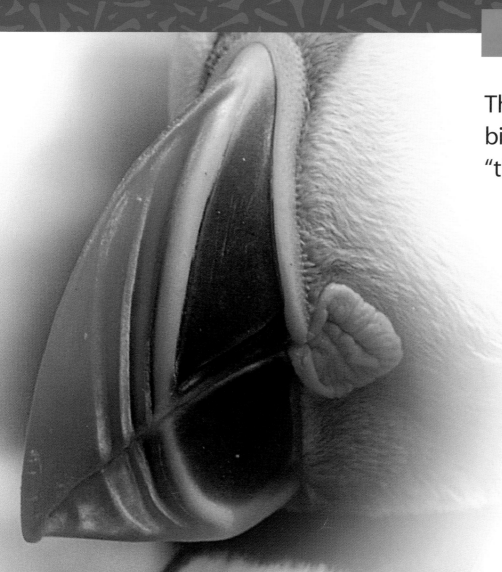

This puffy beak belongs to a bird that some people call "the clown of the sea."

Puffins dive deep and catch
fish with their beaks.
A puffin can hold up
to thirty fish in its beak
at one time. It feeds some
of the fish to its young.
A puffin chick eats more
than two thousand fish before
it starts catching fish for itself.

Puffin chicks keep their parents
very busy!

You see teeth like these every day. Just look in the mirror!

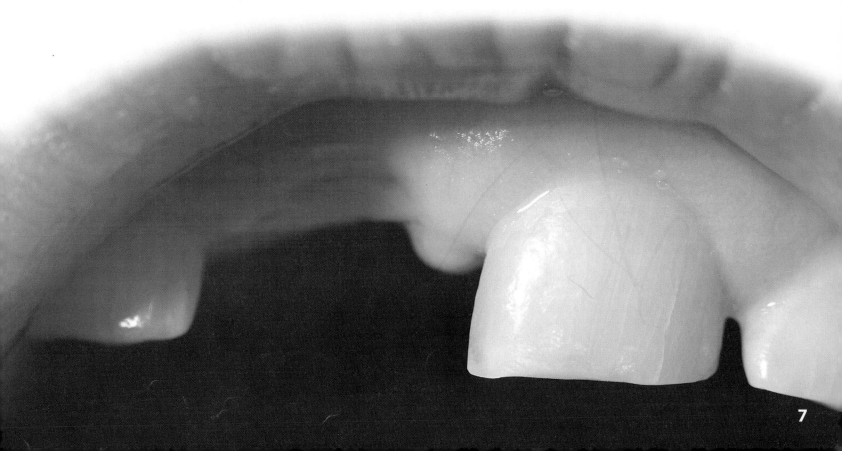

Do you still have all twenty of your baby teeth, or have you lost some?

Inside your gums, adult teeth are starting to grow. They push out your baby teeth. When all of your adult teeth are in, you will have thirty-two teeth. Until then, you may have a few gaps in your smile.

When you feel this hairy tongue on your skin, you probably shoo this bug away.

Shoo, fly, shoo!
A fly's tongue is flat like a pad, but it works like a sponge. Tiny hairs on it soak up food.

Houseflies eat many things that are not clean. A fly's tongue can spread disease. Shoo, fly, shoo!

Do these scary hooks look like a dragon's mouth?

Young dragonflies are called nymphs. They do not fly. Instead, they live under water. A dragonfly nymph has a long lower lip. At the end of the lip are two sharp hooks. The nymph catches food, such as tadpoles, with these hooks.

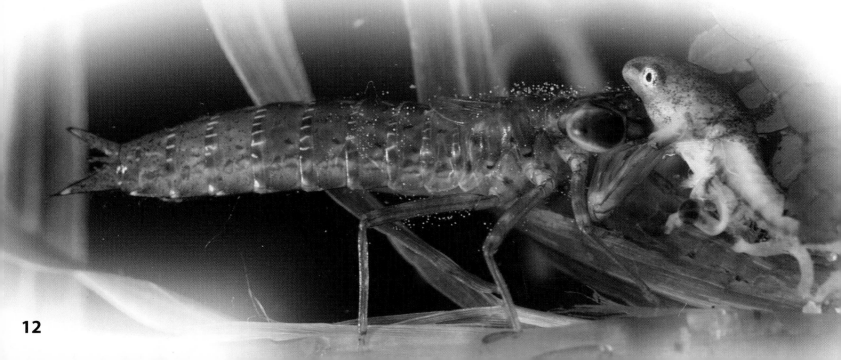

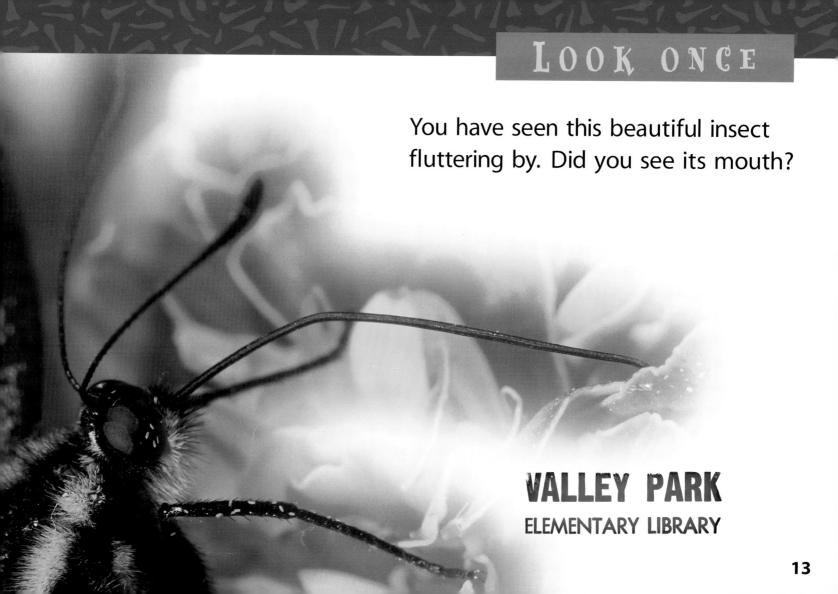

You have seen this beautiful insect fluttering by. Did you see its mouth?

A butterfly curls its tongue under its head. The tongue is called a proboscis. To drink from a flower, the butterfly uncurls its proboscis and uses it like a straw.

14

This animal is famous for changing colors.
It is also famous for its long, sticky tongue.

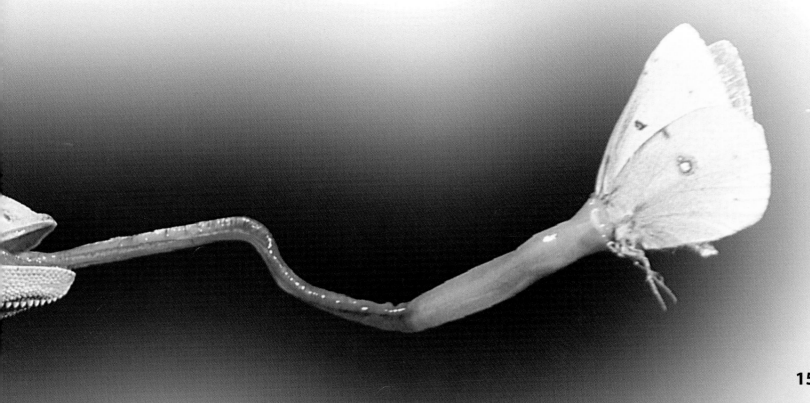

Chameleons are slow on their feet but fast with their tongues. A chameleon's tongue is almost as long as its body. There is sticky mucus at the tip. The tongue shoots out faster than your eye can see. Zzzaap! The chameleon has its meal.

Keep your fingers and toes away from this mouth!

The caiman looks like and is related to the alligator. Caimans and alligators have sharp, pointed teeth. The teeth are built for grabbing and tearing food. Caimans and alligators swallow big chunks of food but do not chew them. They do not often bite people, but don't take chances!

A.

B.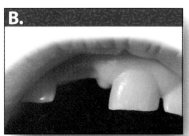

C.

D.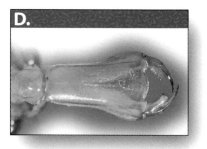

E.

F.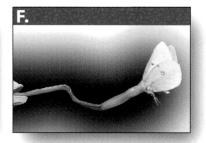

G.

Look closely. Do you know whose mouths these are?

LOOK AGAIN

A.

Puffin

B.

Human child

C.

Housefly

D.

Dragonfly nymph

E.

Butterfly

F.

Chameleon

G.

Caiman

How many were you able to identify correctly?

baby teeth: the first set of teeth that a human has. Baby teeth are replaced by adult teeth as the child grows older.

beak: the hard mouthpart of a bird that extends outward; a bird's bill.

caiman: a type of reptile from Central and South America that is related to alligators and crocodiles.

chameleon: a small lizard that can change its color, or camouflage itself, to blend in with its surroundings.

chick: a young chicken or other bird.

disease: an illness; a condition that keeps the body from being healthy.

gap: a space or opening in something.

gums: the firm, pinkish flesh around the base of the teeth.

mucus: a slippery substance that moistens and protects the nose, throat, and tongue.

nymph: a stage in the life cycle of some insects before they become adults.

proboscis: the mouthpart of a butterfly or other insect that is used to feed on nectar.

puffin: a seabird that has a short neck and a large, often colorful beak.

puffy: puffed out and rounded; full.

shoo: to scare or chase away.

tadpole: a young, newly hatched frog that lives in the water and has a tail.

ACTIVITIES

It Fits the Bill!

Bird beaks come in many different shapes and sizes. Puffins have large beaks that are perfect for catching fish from the ocean. Warblers have very small beaks with which they catch insects. Look in a bird book or on the Internet and compare different kinds of bird beaks. Can you guess what each bird eats by looking at the shape of its beak?

What Beautiful Teeth You Have!

Look in a mirror, and open your mouth wide. Count how many teeth you have. Do you still have all of your baby teeth — twenty in all? When you are an adult, you will have thirty-two teeth. Some animals have even more teeth than humans. The opossum, which is about the size of a cat, has fifty teeth!

Bigmouth Gator

Fold a piece of dark green or brown construction paper in half, the long way. With an adult's help, cut the paper along the fold, so there are two long, narrow pieces. Fold one piece in half, so that the short sides touch. Cut this piece out to form the mouth of your alligator. Cut out small triangles of white paper, and glue them into the mouth as teeth. Glue the mouth section to the front of the long piece of construction paper. Cut out a tail. Add details, such as eyes, with a marker.

Leaping Lizards!

Visit a zoo that has chameleons and other types of reptiles. Notice the mouths of the various reptiles. Do all of them have long tongues for catching food, like the chameleon?

More Books to Read

Alligators and Crocodiles. Michael George (Child's World)
Butterflies. The New Creepy Crawly Collection (series). Graham Coleman (Gareth Stevens)
Chameleons: Masters of Disguise. Secrets of the Animal World (series). Eulalia García (Gareth Stevens)
Dragonflies. The New Creepy Crawly Collection (series). Heather Amery (Gareth Stevens)
How Many Teeth? Paul Showers (HarperCollins)
Insects. Under the Microscope (series). John Woodward (Gareth Stevens)
Teeth. Henry Arthur Pluckrose (Franklin Watts)

Videos

Butterflies. (Coronet, The Multimedia Co.)
Chameleons. (New Dimension Media)
The Dragonfly. (Barr Films)

Web Sites

magicnet.net/~mgodwin/
starbuck.ced.appstate.edu/schools/Lenore/b/dragon.html

Some web sites stay current longer than others. For further web sites, use your search engines to locate the following topics: *alligators, butterflies, chameleons, dragonflies, puffins,* and *teeth.*

INDEX